THE APE WITH THE THREE KILOGRAMME BRAIN

Andrew Chambi

authorHOUSE®

AuthorHouse™
1663 Liberty Drive
Bloomington, IN 47403
www.authorhouse.com
Phone: 1-800-839-8640

First published by AuthorHouse   12/07/2011

ISBN: 978-1-4678-7938-5 (sc)
ISBN: 978-1-4678-7939-2 (ebk)

THE APE WITH THE THREE KILOGRAMME BRAIN

"If we do not initiate the young into the village, they will burn it down to feel the warmth." **African proverb.**

THE ILLITERATE SCHOLAR

The hoard swayed gently as if a field of corn, swaying in the wind. This was humanity at its best—waiting patiently in solemn silence for their loved ones to appear from the belly of the steel eagle. Where out in daily life, a lover may have spent hours in monastic solitude, absorbed by work or the latest game or a documentary, here, they all made the effort to stand on tip toes in anticipation. Television screens offered facts about delays and arrivals: worshiped like altars. Even the taxi drivers: effectively paid, temporary lovers and family, found it within their depths to fathom a smile.

Within half an hour, as orders dictated, the whole airport would be transformed, on account of the arrival of the country's premier politician: Prime Minister Smyth. As the first non-Etonian to reside in Downing Street for over fifty years, the citizens of its country rejoiced in glorious expectation: in recent history, and certainly as far back as anyone could remember, the state had been run by over-privileged, over-funded clowns, who took every opportunity to fill their bellies and their bank accounts with blood money from the declaration of wars, raising of taxes, bribes from media moguls and aiding of corporations. The country united behind Smyth because of the general poverty, lack of opportunities and the promise that a man from the same starting blocks as everyone else would see the need for change.

Change: there's a funny word. Held like a badge of honor by the down trodden beggars that line the streets, seeking a short term solution to their empty stomachs. Eyes glazed with hunger and the memory of a warm bed and a loving touch. The silent dirty secret of the wealthy cities. Buy or be bought. But these poor souls are too devastated to be demanding the sort of change that would take them out of the gutters. They are well past that point. They are so distant from the society their streets line. They are past the politics of the rich or social care of the poor. They care not for the red or blue dress; medium or super spicy curry at the latest trendy, overpriced restaurant. The change they speak of is the stuff most throw away, mainly because it weighs down the pockets. The paper of any real value is not for them. To the functioning member of society, beggars change is what is used to pay for parking a car or for tips in a restaurant. To the forgotten under belly, change is a meal, a drink or some warm, muddy liquid, called coffee—holy temporary respite, before the cold kicks in again. A change from the pain and degradation of the paving stones. A chance to sooth the growls of an angry belly . . .

But I digress . . .

Back at the airport, the scenes of moments ago had changed. Within minutes of the instructions being distributed through the ranks, the public were cleared out and armed police guards took position. Due to social climate and political pressure, this was the first Premier politician not to use a private jet for business, thus sparing the public purse over half a million in annual fees! Token gestures such as these were seen as a sure sign that this state educated candidate would shrug off the veil of hypocrisy and would finally address the intense corruption that plagued this country and its leaders. For the moment, the intense social issues surrounding his leadership and the state would have to take a dominant backseat. Mainly because at precisely the moment in question, large groups of young people had congregated in the capital's parks and open spaces to demand what they felt was theirs: a stake in society; a state funded health system; an education system which provided equal opportunities and jobs that paid enough to provide for a family.

"Sir, the group has congregated again—The police are asking how to deal with them."

During the 1980s and 2010s, peaceful protests had turned into scenes of riots and it was of paramount importance that memories of those days would not be stirred. As a direct result of civil unrest, the country had billions knocked off market valuations and millions spent on the clear up. Buildings burnt and communities torn apart. The PM knew it would be essential to stop these thugs, or run the risk of his legacy being ruined.

"Is it a peaceful meeting?" Smyth enquired.

"For the moment . . ."

"Well then, who cares . . . ? Let them vent some frustration. But do keep an eye on things."

The PM gave off the appearance of being a peaceful man; essentially one who wanted the best for his people, he had advised the media that he believed it was their right to express their opinions as long as they observe the law. After all, an opinion was what differentiated man from beast. To deny a man of his opinion was akin to imprisonment: Imprisonment of the mind and soul . . . This thought bought a wry smile to his dry lips. He recorded the phrase on his Dictaphone.

Admittedly, the economy may not have been performing to its full potential, but the state health system had recently received full sponsorship from Insurehealth—which provided globally unrivalled health care. Abolition of state education replaced by privately funded academies had yielded wonderful results; ensuring schooling for all and attracting international companies to buy a stake in the education system. McDonalds had recently opened its school of fine cuisine securing both a large amount of international attention and funding for the public purse. All was good despite the minority and their persistent protests.

As his gaunt silhouette filed the doorframe of the arrivals lounge, the camera flash rounds went off as if ordered to fire at will. After a quick wave and the customary picture with a clueless, bewitched baby, he was chauffeured home. From the back of the car, the premier was able to get straight back to business.

After a video conference with the minister of education, informing him of the (recently privatized) armies' intention to open a military academy and a quick word with Downing Street's chef about the evening's choice of cuisine, he sat back to enjoy a glass of fine French wine.

He wound down the window, which separated the driver from him and offered: "Charles, what are your thoughts on these meetings in the capital?"

"Meetings?" Charles returned "what meetings?"

"The ones in the city. I've yet to see any news reports, but there are planed protests today. The police are dealing with it, but they are claiming lack of social support and equality . . . they want opportunities. Everyone wants opportunities! That's why people go to university—where did you go uni?"

"I went to Newcastle. Unfortunately, funding evaded me during my second year, but after saving up enough, I managed to get a first class degree in law . . . a few years after that, I was lucky enough to find myself driving for your good self, Sir."

"I see . . ." Smyth had stopped listening soon after he had started. On his small in-built computer, he was seeing live reports of groups of angry young men and women. Banners demanded opportunity, social care and fair education glinting against the sun.

The benevolent politician furrowed his brow. He didn't understand how after a great deal of reform, after they had attracted the largest international companies—in all sectors—and after the fanfare of his election, the people wanted more. Where the once crumbling public health system creaked and groaned under the strain of an increasingly unhealthy public, the country now boasted top hospitals and top doctors—for those who could afford it . . . Well, it was all free at the point of delivery.

The sharp shrill of his personal phone line interrupted his thoughts: "yes?"

"Sir, are you aware of the developments occurring in the city?"

"The protests?"

"Yes sir, they are headed for the worst. Shop windows have been broken and groups are attacking the police."

"Hmmm . . . let the police deal with it. Keep me informed of any developments as they occur."

What an ungrateful mob—he thought to himself—as the phone cut the air again with its high pitch shriek.

"Yes?"

"Sir, the CEO of Initio-clean has been on the phone. He claims the contract with his company did not cover any cleaning after civil disorder. It would require a re-negotiation to deal with this scale of operation."

"Tell him we will be dealing with the issue later—if riots break out—which they won't. Don't tell him that-assure him the police are optimistic this will be a peaceful protest. They will deal with any disturbances before they break out. But also tell him that we are currently in talks with other companies about the renewal of that contract. Keep him on his toes."

"Of course sir."

Despite very healthy donations to Smyth's personal charities, it had not been written in stone that he should offer exclusive access to those contacts! With the privatization of social care, justice system, military and the job centers; corporations asking for greater powers and the media in support, it was time. Time to keep his promises to his most fruitful supporters.

Abolition of the archaic anti-monopoly laws.

CERAMIC THUMBS

A few months later, whilst the PM dined with one of his sons—a secret child, resulting from an unfortunate event in Thailand—a layer of dust had formed, deep enough for the ant scuttling past to leave a trail of tiny six dotted tracks, from one side of her face to the other. Violet had been assured since her conception that she was one of the last of her kind: beautiful, delicate and soothing to hold. She was among the old mans most prized possessions and had been since his mother-her original owner—had died. Despite rarely leaving her shelf, other than to be admired by a passing customer, Violet was one of the few that still took an active interest in the state of society. The old man would often glance at her during the evening news and could swear the tear on her porcelain face had run a little further or a new tear had formed, as if by magic.

An electrician by trade, the old man would gently cradle her in his overworked hands and admire the precision of his late mothers stitching. Just after she died, he used to confide in Violet, as she always kept her opinions to herself: a faint smile betraying her compassion and fading eyes conveying her weariness. His mother had made her over 100 years ago—as a way of occupying her then juvenile mind. It was an attempt to block out the political backdrop of the time and the war that would eventually be referred to as the Second World War.

Violet had witnessed a century of social regression, corruption and privatization; and though she may not have been the most intellectual member of society, she knew it was no accident that the rise of the superstar coincided with a once new social phenomenon. Instant self-gratification had first seeped and now gushed thought the bolted doors of the working class. And who could blame them? With live feeds of politicians, sports, music and film stars giving into their whims at the drop of a hat, buying planes, islands and friends, who could blame the silent majority for wanting more? Job centers closed; Universities charging what would amount to ten years on the average wage; No national health system and a plethora of other social change, social mobility had effectively come to a standstill.

She had observed a steady progression over the last few decades which, at first, the people heartedly accepted—due to its convenience, but had later come to smother the very fabric of society. She had observed large corporations grow from convenience stores to supermarkets to hypermarkets. The range of goods they offered grew and grew, whilst the prices they offered fell. Groceries, clothes, electric appliances, communication devices insurance, loans and today "anything that exists" is part of the familiar promise. The companies that often provided greatest convenience also provided a homologous and consistent product. It also provided great profits to the very fortunate few that pulled the strings. By the turn of the century, several of these great companies had accessible assets in value far greater than even the most powerful country. Where once seen as a threat to society, they had now been awarded the title of state sponsor. Providing them with the power not just too officially influence state policy, but to be the dominant force; to out compete any other.

Where there was once some choice over where to spend wages, shops now stretched across boroughs and streets, giving entire areas an identity and a slogan. Where people used to quote post codes as their badge of honor, they now identified with a logo and a bargain. Gone were the days of the independent record shop selling old vinyl, or the cafe owned by the sweet old Turkish couple, where a smile was more valuable than any denomination of coin or note.

Today, hypermarkets stretch as far as the eye can see offering "anything that exists". Food, holidays, information. Today the independent shop is a thing of the past. There are no aspirations of starting your own business because all business has been taken care of. Even new ideas are soon bought out by the monopolies. The sweet, hardworking, economic cogs have had their teeth worn flat and have been replaced.

The old man's shop is one of very, very few to remain . . .

The ring of the shop doorbell interrupted Violets eternal internal monologue.

A stout, ginger man filled the frame of the door and peered through the small gap in the steel shutters that smothered the entrance, whilst the old man shuffled his way to open up. The door was rarely left open owing to the vandals and thieves, but even encounters like those did not fill the old man with hate, as it had most. He was always quick to remind anyone to curse them of the lack of opportunities that remained, the closure of job centers and private sale of council housing.

The customer gingerly entered the shop. His eyes glazed in awe as he lapped up the sights on the surrounding shelves. Ancient computers, TVs, radios, gizmos and gadgets. As a smile invaded his frosty face, he asked: "I've never seen this shop before! How long has it been here?"

"My father opened it over 80 years ago! I've been working here for as long as I can remember."

"I've never seen anything like it! Do you only sell electronics?"

"Yes"

"That is amazing!"

At that point, his eyes wondered over the dusty corner of Violet's shelf.

"Is that a doll?" He asked, picking her up. "She is beautiful! . . . I've only ever these in old films, and even then, never as pretty as this."

"She was made by my mother, nearly a hundred years ago. She's certainly not for sale, but I'm glad you like her."

After an hour of conversation, the ginger man hastily shook the old man's hand.

"So I've modified the TV set: it's now able to receive all channels and I've replaced the circuit that is well known for shorting. I can't offer any of the other conveniences like the big shops, but you are welcome to bring it back if it gives you any trouble."

With a "thank you so much!" and a genuine smile, the ginger man picked up his TV set and left.

That is why the old man had persevered, Violets internal monologue continued, despite the hypermarket's best efforts to close his shop. He cared. Put simply, he had a stake in his business. Something a daunted hypermarket employee could never feel . . .

A few days passed and a few micro meters more dust had collected. By now, anyone tracking the ant would have had difficulty reading its tracks. But Violet was also bored. So bored, she had taken to counting the pixels on the screen which was opposite her—she would assure you this is a harder task than you can imagine. Either way, it beat trying to twiddle ceramic thumbs.

Three days had passed since the ginger man had bought his TV and Violet was concerned about affairs closer to home. Although the streets where often filled with people, they were not the types who came into the shop for trade. She had observed, over time, that there are many different types of people. Some are on the television and they often have nice possessions and are reported on by the news. Some people are connected, like the old man and Violets maker, by a bond called family. Some people, which she did not have much experience of-other than a few unfortunate incidences involving the shop and eventually the arrival of the police-were called thieves, thugs . . . Actually, there were a lot of words used to describe these people. And these people did not often act in nice ways. Violet also knew that some people were children and she loved these more than all.

The very cotton fibers in her torso creaked in an attempt to call the child to pick her up when one came into the shop. It had been six months since that had happened last. In fact it had been twenty three years since a child had even looked at her. In the early years, she was often admired but first she lost favor with the fixations of fashion and then hand held computers and TV screens demanded the attention of the eyes of an entire generation. For now, the only people that passed the shop were the sort the old man would never dream of opening up to. The types that was filthy and usually pissed. The types that could often be seen stealing from some dazed boy's rucksack whilst it hangs off his stumbling body or beating up a hyper market security guard for a bottle of vodka.

Two more days passed and no sight of the old man, but Violet had started worrying after the first: he was always tinkering with some gizmo our other in the back of the shop. Even on Sundays he would have the screw driver or soldering iron in the back of some appliance, trying to resurrect it. Thinking about it, the last she had seen of him was when he had received a phone call for which he ran down stairs into the shop, night gown flailing, answered, had a heated conversation and shuffled back upstairs. That was until now, when he ran again down the stairs, overcoat slung over his shoulder and a small bag dragged behind him. He shuffled straight past her towards the front door and stopped as his hand reached for the lock. He paused for what felt like an eternity to all concerned, but was in actual fact no more than a few second at most, turned around and walked back towards the counter. He came to stop just in front of the shelf on which Violet sat. He gently picked her up and wiped off the layer of dust from her face. The ant could never be tracked now.

"I could never leave you behind." He said softly, almost to himself. And stuffed her into the already over packed bag in between a pair of pants and some socks. With that, he paced over to the bolted door, unlocked it, drew the shutters and left without bothering to lock it.

PINK PRAWN

The voice sounded more distorted the longer it went on. Each vowel seemed to be held for longer, as the image of the slap head-crowned-suit slid more out of focus. Michael was falling asleep. In a meeting. It was hardly impressive stuff. As he consciously forced himself back to reality, the source of the voice came sharply into focus. Pacing back and forth like some sort of Human pendulum –timekeeper of Everycare—was Ben Armstrong. The Boss. Unable to take it anymore, Michael excused himself from the meeting—mumbling something about going to the gents' room—and made for the lift. As he passed Deb's desk, the heavy fumes from her steaming cup of coffee grasped his nostrils, with a vice-like grip. They almost recoiled in disapproval at the stench, until each cell in his body recalled what the potent muddy liquid could do. Caffeine. He longed for the chemical buzz it unleashed when it hit the pit of his stomach. The growing sense of panic, as guzzle after guzzle, the lungs first coerce and eventually burn in a bid to take in some fresh air.

The doors pulled apart with a loud ping, followed by a laborious metallic groan. Before hitting the G button, a used newspaper, left behind on the reception coffee table caught his eye. The headline read "Wide-scale riots expected in the capital: night three". On the way down, he couldn't stop thinking about the implications of the headline. On the street, rain fell. He looked up toward the sky from the shelter of the building entrance. The clouds were low and dense. They stretched from one end of the horizon to the other. Michaels mind started wondering, as it often does. He thought about the clouds and the water, and getting drenched on the way to the shop. When he got there, he picked up two cans of the cheapest taurine-based caffeine drink. Pink Prawn. The ancient man behind the desk laid his hand expectantly on the table without even acknowledging Michaels dripping frame. Two coins placed in the crusted Asian palm: transaction complete.

Water was still falling from the sky when Michael took to the streets again. Looking woefully at his watch, he decided at that point that going back to work would be impossible. The feeling of pins and needles invading his arse muscles seemed like a fate cast in hellfire. Taking a sly left turn just before his office, Michael headed down towards the river—he would leave his car at work and return to pick it up when the work day ended, rousing less suspicion. A slow walk along the bank normally sorted his head out; being stuck in a

9-5 office job certainly didn't help his current state of mind. The former artistic ramblings in his journal had lately turned into the laments of a disillusioned fool. Moving to the city from the remote country settings of his university had had an effect on him similar to a magician whipping the tablecloth off the ornately dressed table . . . Except all the tableware broke.

He had started working at the company after he had finished his degree. Back in those days, most people went to university, so most jobs demanded more than just a degree—at least three years' experience too. Where Michael's older siblings had secured jobs with college qualifications, the entire subsequent generation was urged to attend higher education, in order to satisfy the privatized institution's insatiable appetite for profit. Over time, as 80% attended uni to do some course or other, including pop studies and DJing degrees, employers began to question the relevance of these courses, as well as the more traditional ones. When newly qualified doctors were more interested in which car the TV stars were driving than in their own profession, the private employers tightened their fists—demanding not just qualifications but experience too. This created an interesting catch twenty-two. Where a newly qualified student graduated, they were unable to find employment in their field due to the lack of three years' experience, which could of course only be achieved by being employed—which is what they were trying to do in the first place.

He cracked open and downed the first can of Pink Prawn—he felt "the rush of the ocean, in your mouth". He also felt his heart rate double within a minute as the synthetic adrenaline made its way through his stomach lining, flowed through capillaries and arteries until it found itself to various synapses. Here, it fulfilled its designer's intention and provided an intense biological turbo charge, which is what was making the hair on the back of Michaels neck stand on end.

Logically, a job's purpose is to provide money which is needed to buy things to survive. When bills need to be paid, money is money and a job is a job, so people started to take whatever jobs were available. And they did end up with three years' experience. Working in an unrelated profession to their degree, unable to progress in that profession because of a lack of relevant qualifications, they got stuck on the bottom rung of the ladder. So it transpired; the university degree lost its value. Reserved now, since full privatization, for the fortunate few that can afford the extortionate fees . . . Mind, it is all free at the point of delivery.

Though Michael had spent a while searching-in vain-for a job after uni, through the usual means: internet and the job center, he remained unemployed for six months.

By which point he decided to swallow his pride and ask his uncle for a job at Everycare— "where your EVERY need is taken CARE of". He knew it was not as bad as he made it out to be: they offered a 8% discount to all employees and 15% to senior members of staff, all were offered a place in the company dormitory for general employees and senior members got a company house and car, all staff were invited to the state of the art artificial company sea front, for an unlimited amount of time (within the 20 day holiday allowance): located just five minutes bus ride from the dorms whilst the privileged few had access to the company island resort, accessible only by private jet. Michael was lucky. He was slotted into a recently vacant senior position that had no relevance to his anthropology degree. Where opportunities were as rare as time travel, a bit of nepotism never hurt anybody.

He downed the next can. His pupils dilated again and his scrotum shriveled a little more.

As he turned the corner to cross the foot bridge that led to a pedestrian highway, in the direction of his house, he saw a pair of police people pacing towards him looking paranoid. He stopped walking toward them when they started waving and pointing in the opposite direction to which he was going. He couldn't make out what they were saying but they clearly looked a bit distressed. By the time they had caught up to him, he had the jist of the situation. Apparently large groups of youths were gathering in the business district in angry protest. Police had just been ordered to close paths leading south of the river. Back to work with Michael it was. Like a stream to the sea, he felt like he couldn't avoid it. Striding confidently back into the conference room, he acknowledged Ben's eagle eyes, waved his phone in the air and sprinkled the magic word: "family", with a severe shake of the head as if to shake off an angry wasp, sat back down in his chair at the large oval desk. A deck of suits; dealt to each chair around the table.

As his cheeks nestled back into their familiar dents in the leather, he picked up his Mont Blanc pen and opened his planner to the last page. He desperately needed to get back with the flow of the meeting. His uncle had already been having words with him about his performance.

" . . . so what is the final figure?" Ben demanded.

They all knew it was good. They had spent the last thirty years engineering the markets to be so. Recently, it had been very good. Very very good. As the opposing parallel rows all craned their spectacled heads towards the accounts director, Ben took an off-the-hook shot at the ring with the mini-basketball.

"YES" Ben roared, punching the air and squinting: when the ball passed through the net without touching the side.

"As you can see in the report, profits are up. Quite a lot on this time last year." The accounts manager let out a school-girls squeal. "I got off the phone just before the meeting. I'm reliably informed that last year, we made three times in profit the amount that all four superpowers made in tax and other revenues in the same year. That is after we have had to pay all tax, fines, fees and other royalties to them."

The table erupted with applause and congratulatory chat. When every back had been sufficiently patted, and the giggles contained to smirks, the meeting took to its previous format.

"So where are we able to improve? How do we keep profits shooting?!" Ben roared at his crowd.

"Our electronics department in the South west is not performing any better. We have implemented all procedures discussed: surveillance, out pricing, active marketing and even the more personal approach, but the problem persists."

"How does that little bastard do it?"

Over the last decade, large corporations had spent millions on a long term campaign, in a bid to ensure they receive the maximum commerce available. This entailed, among other things, eliminating all competition on the high street. Small shops like the old mans were proving to be very troublesome. They just couldn't work out why a handful of small businesses persisted despite aggressive competition and intelligent market maneuvers. Admittedly, there weren't many left, perhaps 500 independent shops nationally; still, this was not good enough for the giants.

"I've read posts on a website about this, but you hear so much rubbish these days." One of men with a nose reminiscent of a vulture's beak squawked enthusiastically.

"What have you read?"

"Well, apparently—and I trust the source—funds have been finding their way into certain charities accounts. Charities associated with certain people. Funds from—and they checked—the owners of many of the companies we have been . . . leaning on."

"Hmmm . . ." Ben paused. "This might not be such a bad thing."

"These companies are essentially being protected by the government! How is that a good thing? Our long term aim is . . ."

"I set that aim-you tit . . ." Ben's fat hands clamped onto the back of the chair he had been leaning against. He squeezed it until his knuckles changed colour from red to white. The room of men, listed among the most influential men in their industry, squirmed in their chairs like naked chicks, caught unaware in their nest." . . . Has this information been made public?"

"Not to the general public."

"Leak it." Ben sneered.

Michael's ears perked up. "But sir, if the public find out, they will burn them all to the ground!"

Ben looked at the source of the disturbance. "End of meeting". And left.

*　　*　　*

Later on that evening, the tires on Michael's car crunched their way over his long gravel drive. The remainder of his day had consisted of another two meetings with store managers and the obligatory lunch with his uncle. They had dined at the in-store Greek restaurant, which consisted of the usual mezes and the unexpectedly pleasant waitress, which made the experience all the more pleasurable for them both. Back at the house, Michael was enjoying siting in his newly installed steam room. When his body had decided it could take no more, he made his way to the full-body mirror in his en suite bathroom and examined his physique.

Throughout his adolescence, school peers had given him a hard time about his rotund features. This in turn had made our young protagonist quite paranoid about his looks—as so often happened to the young members of our society. Where he should have spent his university life experimenting in an entirely new, and quite unique social environment, Michael did his upmost to blend into the background, smirking away from any opportunity to engage in conversation with any of the fine three kilogramme brains that he met. Any time he was introduced, a quick "hi" and hand shake would suffice, leaving the jokes, conversation and inevitably any sexual encounters to his socially confident friend. When he noticed his friend sneak off around the corner for a more appropriate level of privacy, Michael would usually take this as his cue to slink home. Apart from one time.

One night, when the two friends were frequenting their usual haunt, a first year student—confident as she was pretty—strode up to them. She glanced at them both but unusually, her eyes settled on the normally invisible Michael. After a brief introduction, she took Michael by the hand and led him to her dormitory room. That was Michaels first and last experience of the dating game-if it in any shape resembled "the dating game". From there, when they had both finished their studies, they moved in together, got engaged and were now waiting for their big day to arrive. That first encounter took place almost a decade ago and since then Becca, his wife-to-be, had ensured he lost his pot-belly and generally any excess, unwanted podge. She had put him on a strict diet which eliminated any carbohydrates and made sure he stuck to it. She also put him on an exercise routine to match any Olympian. The steam room was one of her last steps in a strategically planned, almost military assault on Michael's love handles.

That evening, dinner consisted of a flat-packed microwave meal—a break to the usual restaurant meal. Michael bared his recently polished teeth in a grin—proud of his cardboard box meal. She in turn smiled back—not betraying her thoughts.

"Can we eat in front of the TV babe?" she asked.

"But I spent ages setting up the dining room!" The candles glinted through the frosted glass door to the kitchen.

"I know—and I appreciate it, but I'd like to be comfortable with you tonight . . . let's sit on the sofa" a gentle touch to the shoulder and a peck on the cheek confirmed her intentions—Michael had no choice.

With dinner eaten, containers disposed of, and forks in the dishwasher, the young couple sunk into each other's arms and settled down for the evening. Moving pictures entertaining their complex brains so that no conversation would ever need to take place. Stories of joy, hate, love and pain. Mundane stories, funny stories and celebrity news. The happy couple, much like most people alive today spends their entire life surrounded by friends and family they will never get to know. Distracted by heavily edited stories and abstract animated games. A species sedated by flickering images and synthetic sound.

The new opiate of the masses.

Sleepy thoughts and a warm duvet gently crossing their mind and the faint glow of the TV in the background. Fiona's eyes gently cracked open in time for images of the Everycare advert to stream through.

"OH! It's Johnny from Marketing!" She perked up. Johnny was posing in front of the newly open store at the airport.

"Hhmmmm?" Michael had fallen into a deeper sleep.

"Oh, sorry, nothing." She hadn't meant to wake him . . . but it was too late.

By the time he had slightly opened his eyes, the image had already fallen onto his retinas and his hyperactive brain had already translated it as a threatening image. Having caught Johnny from marketing taking a midnight stroll with a suspiciously drunk Becca at last year's Christmas party had left a sour taste in Michael's mouth.

The relaxed, jovial mood from a few hours ago dissolved into the ether. Michael stumbled to his feet unable to take his eyes off his partner. The familiar glare, tainted with hints of jealousy, pain and anger.

Of the silent cacophony occurring in his head, the one emotion crystallizing into actual thought was a warning. A warning from the depths of his conscience: "do not hit her". After catching her last Christmas, things got a little bit out of hand and physical. Something Michael will always regret. With a mental restriction in place, he needed to find another way to vent the volcanic, explosive anger he was feeling.

In a fit of rage he planted his left heel into the center of the screen. Right into Johnny's smug, grinning face.

When the sparks had died down and the yelps and cries had faded. The couple took three deep breaths before their eyes met.

At first his mind was blank. The mute TV punctuated the silence of the situation and Michael realized what a big mistake he had made when she eventually said: "We need to talk."

❉   ❉   ❉

Keeping up a professional exterior, the next day at work felt smeared with of guilt for Michael. He was so rarely aggressive and knew it was no excuse, but knew that something was going on. So he geared himself up for another day of square walls and paperwork. Type, shuffle and shift . . . Or at least that was the plan until he heard a series of screams and shouts coming from down the corridor.

Through the glass pane on which the giant Everycare logo was mounted, that overlooked the front lobby of the office lobby, Michael saw swarms of people filing into the building. None of them wore the familiar, smart three pieces that normally littered the corridors they wore athletic suits. They were a collection of different ethnicities and ages. Men and women, adult and child. United by tracksuits.

Michael didn't want to hang about to find out what was going to happen. He made for the nearest fire escape and ran. Taking two steps at a time, he was on the ground floor in a matter of seconds. Opening the emergency escape door set of a high pitched shrill which resonated in his brain in harmony with the bright white light that penetrated through the crack of the door and forced pupils to dilate.

He took to the streets, avoiding streets where he saw large congregations of people. His flailing tie giving him away to some of them who would chase him for a few hundred meters yelping and yelling "GET THE SUITS!" before getting distracted, turning their attention to some other opportunity to loot.

Upon reaching a quiet area, Michael made use of a vacant bench. He took the weight off his heavy feet and heard his heart pounding in his chest. He couldn't figure out what had happened to the city he had once proudly called home . . . Where had all these riots come from? Why had the news not mentioned them?

On the opposite side of the street, a tired silhouette shuffled its way round the corner. Its jagged steps made slow but definite progress until it revealed itself to belong to an old man dragging a small, stuffed bag behind him. The old man had made it half way down the street, when Michael noticed a more ominous shadow form behind him. A mob.

Foreseeing the future, he dashed towards the old man. Michael took him by the arm and whispered "Keep walking: there's a mob behind us and they're going for anyone in a suit. Come with me."

AN INTANGIBLE CONCEPT

Wisps of icy steam rolled off the edge of his lips with each shallow breath. His sunken eyes fixed firmly on the tatty family portrait, precariously hung behind the defunct gramophone. The old boiler had ceased creaking with life over three months ago; and not because it lacked the will. Fuel prices had driven the old man to initially minimize and eventually stop using fossil fuels to heat his house. He had plans for making a generator powered by the electrolysis of water, but the energy he felt during his youth had long drained from his bones. Infected with youth, the old man would have taken up most challenges with the vigor of a buck in mating season—and in most cases succeeded—today, his arthritic frame shuffled about, struggling to make ends meet. Only a shadowy fire lurked in the depths of his eyes, reminiscent of his youthful essence.

The portrait hanging from the nail was a portal to better days. He spent hours wishing he could climb through. To the time when he was surrounded by his family, familiarity and love. The only familiarity he felt today was an empty shop and an empty heart. The old man had noticed a correlation over time between the accumulated wealth of the rich and the down treading of the poor. Backdoor deals and media supremacy result in job loss and violent outbreaks. That is to say, better days were distant, but not distant enough to forget.

For years, people could see the ominous shadow on the horizon but had not acted. Now they all beg for a Robin Hood to deal with their Sheriff of Nottingham. Unfamiliar terms such as "holistic defense measures" or "collateral damage" legitimized unsavory actions had illegitimized a questioning public. With any organizations speaking up for the oppressed branded as terrorists, it soon became the norm to think but not speak. As thought-crimes became more common, thinking became less common until the nation was inhabited by something comparable to cattle.

The chirpy phone smashed its electromagnetic hammer against the bell at fifty hertz, causing the old man's heart to contract painfully in his chest. After a deep breath, he creaked out of his armchair and shuffled his way to the phone; barely lifting his feet to drag them to their next position. Turning the corner on the way down the stairs always made him dizzy for a second recently . . . that couldn't be a good sign.

"Yes minister . . ." Only one person ever called the old man's shop any more: he knew exactly who it was on the other end of the line.

"Ummm . . . Charlie, you need to get out."

"Why? We pay you to protect us from anything."

"Yes, you do . . . did . . . Listen. We're bailing. The military is out of our hands, the police are on strike, the hypermarkets are . . . the hypermarkets! This is a personal call. GET OUT. They've done it. "

The old man cleared his throat.

"Slow down Nick." He demanded.

"It's a bloody civil war out there! We haven't got the man power or the means to stop them and they're going for parliament!! GET OUT NOW! They know about the deals and don't care if you're a one man band or whatever! I'm telling you this because . . . Just please. Come on."

"You're telling me that despite me bowing to demands, paying your charities and . . ."

"It's way past that!! . . . I have to go." Click.

The old man sank into his chair. He had to think. He only had one thought. He needed to get out. The pathetic anticlimax to four generations of a happy loving family home and business.

There was no regular custom at the shop. The ginger man was the last customer, and that was . . . Time has started to blur for the old man. Was it weeks or months? They all blurred into one these days. The hypermarkets were squeezing every business dry, so he had to result to unrealistic means of survival. Hand to mouth and dodgy dealings were the norm. With such infrequent custom, the shop shutters spent more time down and locked than they did up. They also served to protect him from the waves of rioters that had swept down the road sporadically over the last week. It pained him to remember that this was the street that his great grandparents had chosen to buy and call their family home; when properties were affordable. They had come to this country based on its international reputation of fairness and had provided for four generations from its warm embrace. Today its streets are reminiscent of one of the countries to which they themselves would have sent troops to aid in its governing.

He packed his small brief case full of socks, t-shirts and underwear. Two diagrams of electric circuits he had designed and always dreamt of acquiring the parts to make them a reality and small lockable box.

Hoisting the bag up to waist height, he stumbled down the stairs, got to the bottom and slung his overcoat over his shoulder. Dragging his bag behind him, he strode across the shop floor and flicked the switch to raise the shutter. As he raised his hand to unlock the door, a faint, happy memory drifted through his mind. The image of her beautiful, tearful face firmly imprinted on his mind. He turned to the shelf where Violet sat. Her smile as graceful and encouraging as ever. He walked straight towards her, picked her up and wiped the layer of dust that had accumulated on her ceramic face.

He dimly smiled: "I could never leave you behind" under his breath and stuffed her into the small bag.

He paced over to the bolted door, taking in the dusty interior of TVs, radios and clocks one last time, unlocked the door, drew the shutters and left without bothering to lock it.

Outside, the street lamp and a light drizzle illuminated the scene with a dull hew. In an ungraceful panic, the old man punched his arms into the overcoat and made towards the train station. He would miss the sweet childhood memories that the un-kept pavement and the once occupied shops triggered. He would miss the thoughts of his great-grandparents being greeted and welcomed into this country. Offered a life, a business and a means to raise a family.

Pacing at full speed, the old man would have done well to recall that the national train service had been withdrawn a week ago; his eroded neurons were too busy marveling at the fast pace his weary legs had accumulated to allow that to cross his mind.

With just one street to the station, having done well to avoid any hostile mobs, the old man noticed someone sat on a bench further up the street. He was wearing a suit and did not react in a hostile way when their eyes crossed.

"Keep going!" the old man muttered to himself.

Step after step after step. The worst thing about growing old was the fading memories of youth—an intangible concept, confined to grey matter.

Out of nowhere, a gentle hand grasped his elbow—It was the young man from the bench.

"Keep walking: there's a mob behind us and they're going for anyone in a suit. Come with me."

The old man knew he didn't really have much choice. He glanced over his shoulder and saw the crowd in the distance. He was grateful for the help and they made solid progress in the rain; the mob soon disappeared. The young man held onto him very firmly and kept saying things like "there you go" or "you're doing really well", but the old man still didn't know his name. "Michael" came the brief reply and the pair were back on the run. With the old man's frail bones and stiff joints slowing them down and confusion as to exactly what the plan was, the old man stopped Michael and asked.

"Where are we going?"

"I know someone who lives near here. I spoke to them earlier—they mentioned leaving later this evening. I'm hoping we can go with them if they haven't left yet . . ."

"Let's hope so . . ."

With that, Michael took a more solid grip on the old man's elbow—supporting him with an interlocked arm—they progressed further into the city. Both losing track of time and distance: focusing on the safety and warmth of their final destination. They had also unfortunately lost track of the old man's luggage, because if they had taken a moment to peer at it at that point, they would have noticed Violets head and tiny arm slipping out of a crack in the zipper. It almost looked like she was riding a rodeo horse—thrown about by the old mans jagged steps—and just like a rodeo horse rider, she took the fall off her horse with a silent dignity reserved only for the best. The painted tear on her cheek more pronounced than ever as the old man disappeared from her eyes reflection for the last time.

Before the old man could realize the fate of his beloved Violet, he and Michael halted to a stop in front of a set of gates leading to a residential house. There were two luxury business cars secured inside of the gate and what appeared to be discarded boxes, electronics and clothes littering the front yard. Through the window of the car in front, Michael could see a bored child playing on a handheld computer as a panic-stricken man ran out of the house towards the car and threw the two brief cases he was carrying into the boot of the car leading the entourage.

Michael let go of the old man and gripped the drenched gates with both of his hands.

He yelled: "NICK!! Please! It's me, Michael!"

The man stood next to the car, closed the boot and walked over to them. Peering through the gate, the stark imbalance of the situation saturated the wet atmosphere.

Ignoring Michael he asked "Is that you Charlie? It's me, Nick—Commerce Minister—how are you? I haven't seen you in . . . decades!"

The old man's memories stirred. "I spoke to you today."

"That was two days ago, but yes. I told you to get out of here! Why have you left it so long?"

"We are getting out NOW!" Michael interjected. "Please can we get into one of your cars?! You have plenty of room!"

The air was punctuated with a rough "GET 'EM!!", from the far side of the street.

Michael turned to Nick.

"Please! They'll kill us!"

The Minister of Commerce paused . . . . Looked back to his car for a second and then back out to the approaching mob. He looked at the old man and then to Michael.

"If I've learnt one thing with all of this Michael, it's that mixing charity and business is never a good idea."

With that, he paced over to his cars, instructed the drivers, got in and slammed the door shut. The gates opened and the cars made their way out. As he passed Michael, the car slowed down and the window cracked open.

He offered them "Good Luck" and left them to their fate.